UNMUTE YOUR *Heart* WORKBOOK

Survival Kit Tools for Overcoming Domestic Abuse

by Sharon R. Wynn

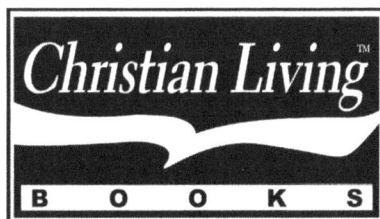

Christian Living™ BOOKS

Christian Living Books, Inc.
Largo, MD

ISBN 9781562293642

Christian Living Books, Inc.
P. O. Box 7584
Largo, MD 20792
christianlivingbooks.com
We bring your dreams to fruition.

Unless otherwise noted, Scripture quotations are taken from the New King James Version®. Copyright© 1982 by Thomas Nelson. Used by permission. All rights reserved. Scripture quotations marked (NIV) are taken from the Holy Bible, New International Version®, NIV®, Copyright©1973, 1978, 1984, 2011 by Biblica, Inc® Used by permission of Zondervan. All rights reserved worldwide. Scripture quotations marked (KJV) are taken from the King James Version of the Holy Bible.

Printed in the United States of America.

CONTENTS

INTRODUCTION

Throughout our lives, we are challenged to forgive, let go, move forward or begin anew. However, as much as we want to and know that it is the best thing to do, we find it challenging. It is much easier said than done. We need support, motivation, and practical instructions to take us where we want to go.

This workbook offers that help. It challenges you to take a closer look naturally and spiritually at the one in the mirror (you). Through the Word of God, it exposes the good and bad in your heart. If we truly want to overcome the worst, we must first be open to hearing from God, deny the flesh, and walk in the Spirit of truth. This allows our healing to take place.

On your spiritual journey, this workbook will give you the tools you need to survive those hard times and help you reach your purpose in life. It enables you to shine the light of God in the dark places of your heart and mind. Moreover, it shows you how to eradicate every bitter, deep-rooted seed and stronghold in your life. Those strongholds may need to be plucked up or brought down in submission to the will of God. This survival kit will aid in beginning that process.

Challenge yourself to open your heart and mind. Be honest and transparent. Ask yourself the tough questions: "why?" and "how?" without fear of expressing what your issues or challenges are. When we look in the mirror, it hides nothing. We see all that we are on the outside to make the necessary adjustments.

In the workbook, there are Core Exercises to engage and challenge you. Key Truths will give you scriptural insight with commentary to encourage you. At the end of each chapter, you will be asked to reflect on the lessons then identify the survival kit tool you can use to activate the transformation taking place within you from the inside out. Prayer sections provide room for you to write your sincere prayer to the Lord. The final section in each chapter is reserved for you to make your own declaration emphatically known even in the face of potential contradiction.

Every beautiful woman who goes through a transformation is being set aside by God, so that He can create something extraordinary inside of her. Although you may feel uncomfortable and crushed in a very dark, lonely place, there is a purpose in the making. This isolated place is where your personal transformation will take place. To observers, it may not look as if much is happening, but God's master plan is at work to bring out the best in you. You will be challenged mentally and emotionally; however, there is always hope.

Some challenges that may surface during your unmuting process may be associated with the abuse and trauma you suffered. Be active in your healing process. Seek a good Christian counselor or someone you love and trust for advice and support. Make sure the person is connected to God and someone to whom you can be accountable. The individual should be able to war with and for you in prayer. Alternatively, find a good, local women's support group in your area to help you sift through your issues. Whatever you do, don't stop fighting.

> For the weapons of our warfare are not carnal but mighty in God for pulling down strongholds, casting down arguments and every high thing that exalts itself against the knowledge of God, bringing every thought into captivity to the obedience of Christ, and being ready to punish all disobedience when your obedience is fulfilled. (2 Corinthians 10:4-6)

BACKPACK CHALLENGE — ARE YOU EQUIPPED?

As you navigate through this workbook, prayerfully search your heart for your truth. Allow the Holy Spirit to reveal to you the tools of healing that you need to apply through His Word. Discover what your backpack is lacking in the natural (backpack survival kit tools). Also, discover what it is missing in the spiritual (fruit of the Spirit and the whole armor of God). Speak positive things and expect a metamorphosis in your life.

Finally, understand how a survival truth will enlighten you and bring you closer to your healing process

TOOLS TO NEVER JOURNEY WITHOUT

The Bible – the infallible Word of God.

Prayer – a solemn request for help or an expression of thanks addressed to God.

The Whole Armor of God – according to Ephesians 6:10-17.

The Fruit of the Spirit – according to Galatians 5:22-23.

SURVIVAL KIT TOOLS

Flashlight - Illumination and Assistance

A flashlight is a small light that can be held in your hand. It is also used for signaling. Sometimes when you are in survival mode, you must signal for help. Remember when you are in distress and everything around you seems dark, use your flashlight. The flashlight represents the Word of God being illuminated in your life. Recall this passage when you are looking for answers:

> Your word is a lamp to my feet and a light to my path. (Psalm 119:105)

Utility Knife - Represents Truth

The utility knife is used for miscellaneous cutting. In your survival kit, your utility knife is truth. Sometimes the truth cuts and hurts. You may not want to hear it when you are barely surviving, and you may not always agree with what is right. However, God knows what is true and right concerning you. Willingly yield yourself to His perfect will.

> For the word of God is living and powerful, and sharper than any two-edged sword, piercing even to the division of soul and spirit, and of joints and marrow, and is a discerner of the thoughts and intents of the heart. (Hebrews 4:12)

👀 Binoculars – Sobriety and Vigilance

Binoculars are used for viewing distant objects. In survival mode, it is imperative that you always stay on guard and be aware of your surroundings.

> Be sober, be vigilant; because your adversary the devil, as a roaring lion, walketh about, seeking whom he may devour. (1 Peter 5:8)

🛏 Blanket and Pillow – Comfort

Blankets are used as coverings and to keep us warm. Pillows provide comfort and protect our heads from the hard, cold ground. During your unmuting season, you will experience many cold and vulnerable moments. When circumstances overwhelm you and you need comfort, recall the following psalm:

> He shall cover you with His feathers, And under His wings you shall take refuge; His truth shall be your shield and buckler. (Psalms 91:4)

⏱ Compass – Direction

The compass is an instrument used for navigation and orientation that shows the direction of a particular location. In survival mode, it is easy to lose your bearings and direction. You may be uncertain what to do, where to turn or even how to identify your current position. You need to hear from God before you make a move.

> Trust in the Lord with all your heart, And lean not on your own understanding; In all your ways acknowledge Him, And He shall direct your paths. (Proverbs 3:5-6)

⛺ Tent – Shelter

Insecurity, fear, and doubt are likely to raise their ugly heads when you are in survival mode. You will definitely need a safe place to rest and feel protected.

> He that dwelleth in the secret place of the most High shall abide under the shadow of the Almighty. I will say of the Lord He is my refuge and my fortress: my God; in him will I trust. (Psalm 91:1-2)

Canteen – Living Water

A canteen is a drinking water bottle designed for hikers and campers. The water it contains keeps them hydrated and energized as they trudge along the rough terrain.

In survival mode, you will experience some tough times. The road may be hard and dreary. You may feel tired, thirsty, and want to give up. But you must stay hydrated to maintain the correct function of every system in your body including your heart, brain, and muscles. At times, your thirst may seem unquenchable. Reach for the living water, Jesus Christ.

> But whosoever drinketh of the water that I shall give him shall never thirst; but the water that I shall give him shall be in him a well of water springing up into everlasting life. (John 4:14)

Backpack – Convenience and Utility

Finally, we always need a bag to carry all of our tools. Backpacks leave our hands free for all the things we need our hands to do. We can reach into our bag whenever we need to use the tool appropriate for the task. When we pack well, we have what we need when we need it.

> Then he took his staff in his hand; and he chose for himself five smooth stones from the brook, and put them in a shepherd's bag, in a pouch which he had, and his sling was in his hand. And he drew near to the Philistine. (1 Samuel 17:40)

CHAPTER 1

TOOLS FOR A SHAKEN REALITY

Food for Thought

In the chapter, "My Reality" of the book *Unmute Your Heart*, I spoke about the challenges I faced accepting that my marriage of 20 years was coming to an end. I was anxious, fearful and had many questions about how I was going to take care of my children. Equally so, I was worried about how to handle my new reality as a single woman and parent. Everything I thought I knew to be true about how my life was supposed to play out was shaken. I was devastated! However, I also experienced a miracle in the pain. I felt God's love and comfort surround me in a special way as only He could. I had no choice but to trust Him. I totally surrendered to Him while my life was spinning out of control – or so I thought.

One day, I got the revelation that God was not finished with me. It was not the end. Rather, it was the beginning of something greater in my life. As time moved on, and I reflected on the mental and emotional toll those many years of abuse had taken on me, I made up my mind to live again. I made the determination to push forward and break through the walls that confined me. I resolved to no longer be a victim. I decided I would no longer feel sorry for my children and myself because of the shame of divorce, abandonment, and even deeper for me, the abuse.

One major reality shaker was having to face the truth that I was a survivor of abuse. I didn't want to believe that it was what it was. I knew it, but I didn't want to own it. The name calling, snatching, hitting, roughing me up, false accusations, and mental abuse were real. I wished it had never happened. I struggled with the thought that it was my fault and somehow, I permitted the abuse. I didn't take action to stop it. Gradually, I realized I was wrong for thinking and feeling that way. I didn't deserve to be treated disrespectfully. I was a valuable woman who deserved to be honored and respected as a wife and mother of five children.

Now, I understand that in life, we have to roll with the punches and be resilient. I will use my pain and experiences to make a difference for someone else. My aim is to touch others, so they can understand they don't have to be defined by what they have been through. You can forgive, be healed, and move forward. I began to experience the hand of God making, molding and healing me on the potter's wheel. He was transforming me from being broken and marred into a beautiful, new creation.

I don't know what has shaken your reality. Maybe it was divorce, the death of a loved one, the loss of employment or homelessness. Whatever it was, our heavenly Father is just a prayer away from restoring and healing you.

🔑 Key Truth #1

> And we know that in all things God works for the good of those who love Him, who have been called according to His purpose. (Romans 8:28, NIV)

You may not understand what you are facing in your life right now, but God has a purpose for you. Your circumstances may look contrary to what God has promised you, but continue to trust Him and watch great things come to pass.

💡 Survival Kit Question #1

Identify an occasion in your life when you felt your reality was shaken. Explain how it may have affected you.

_____

_____

_____

_____

_____

⟦?⟧ Survival Kit Question #2

Knowing the Father loves and cares for you in every situation, how can you exercise faith when circumstances seem insurmountable?

_____

_____

_____

_____

⟦?⟧ Survival Kit Question #3

As believers in Christ, the Word of God is our weapon to combat the Enemy when we face our challenges. How does this ensure a victorious outcome for you?

_____

_____

_____

_____

⟦♥⟧ Core Exercise

Some of us have been hurt by situations that were out of our control. On the other hand, some of us have contributed to our issues, and we are prayerfully seeking God for healing and restoration. List the areas of your life where you are seeking God's healing and restoration.

_____

_____

_____

_____

Backpack Tools

What negative circumstances have impacted your life? Looking back, how has God transformed you for the better?

_____

_____

Moving forward, what survival tools can you use to help you adjust to new and unfamiliar circumstances? (Refer to the tool options in your survival kit.)

_____

_____

_____

_____

WRITE YOUR OWN PRAYER AND DECLARATION

Prayer

_____

_____

_____

_____

_____

_____

_____

Declaration

NOTES:

NOTES:

CHAPTER 2

TOOLS FOR YOUR PROCESS

Food for Thought

Nobody wants to go through a difficult process, but we all want the benefits that the completion of the process yields. In the garden of Gethsemane the night before His death, Jesus prayed to the Father saying:

> Lord let this cup pass. Nevertheless, not my will, but your will be done. (Matthew 26:39)

His prayer was fervent because He realized the process He would soon endure would not only be painful and brutal, but it would separate Him from His Father.

Jesus took all the sins of the world on the cross. Mathew 27:46 records that at that moment, He felt abandoned and asked the Father, "Why has thou forsaken me?" Like Jesus, as you go through your traumatic experiences, you may ask God to remove your pain and brokenness. You may feel as if He has abandoned you. In spite of your loneliness and the excruciating pain, trust God to take you to your next level of anointing. Stay focused, and endure the stormy process. Hold on and let the process develop the greatness within you. You are somebody else's answer. Your experience gives others hope and determination to press forward with the expectation of victory.

🔑 Key Truth #1

In His most vulnerable moments, Jesus was tempted by the Devil three times. However, Jesus was able to combat him with the Word of God. The very last time Jesus was tempted, Satan commanded Him to bow down and worship him in exchange for the world and all its splendors.

> Jesus said to him, 'Away from me, Satan! For it is written: 'Worship the Lord your God, and serve him only. (Matthew 4:10, NIV)

In the preceding verse, we see Jesus using the Word to defeat the Enemy. Likewise, we can defeat Satan with the Word of God. The bottom line is there are no short cuts through the process. You must go through each stage to receive your victory on the other side of your trial. Arming yourself with God's weapons makes you an overcomer. Let's look closely and examine our tools.

🔑 Key Truth #2

Ephesians 6:14 instructs us to gird up our loins with truth. The truth of the Word will expose the issues you hide because they are too painful to confront. The good news is that when you face up to your issues and accept them for what they are, you will find freedom and the healing process can begin. Being afraid to confront your issues prolongs your agony, prevents your deliverance, and stunts your personal growth.

💡 Survival Kit Question #1

Soldiers use breastplates to protect their vital organs. Ephesians 6:19 instructs us to have the breastplate of righteousness in place. How can it protect your heart in the spiritual?

_____

_____

_____

_____

_____

Survival Kit Question #2

Ephesians 6:15 instructs us to keep our feet shod with the preparation of the gospel of peace. As believers, it is our duty to be always ready to represent the God we serve, even when we are going through our painful processes. Why is this important for us to do?

_____

_____

_____

_____

Survival Kit Question #3

Ephesians 6:16 instructs us to take the shield of faith to quench every fiery dart of Satan that attacks us. Why is it vital to maintain faith through your process? What are the benefits?

_____

_____

_____

_____

Survival Kit Question #4

Ephesians 6:17 instructs us to take the helmet of salvation, as well as the sword of the Spirit, which is the Word of God. Explain why it is very important for you to have both pieces of armor in spiritual warfare? How would the helmet and the sword go hand in hand?

_____

_____

_____

_____

Core Exercise

What is a soldier without a weapon on a battlefield? What is a believer without the sword of the Spirit?

> But He answered and said, it is written: 'Man shall not live by bread alone, but by every word that proceeds from the mouth of God.' (Matthew 4:4)

List five reasons why it is important to know and declare the Word of God, as well as the will of God over your circumstances while you are going through your process. What are the benefits of this?

1. _____

2. _____

3. _____

4. _____

5. _____

Backpack Tools

As you go through your process, you cannot fight the Enemy without the whole armor of God. The armor helps you win wars in the spiritual so you can live victoriously in the natural. In your backpack, you are equipped with the tools to fight every battle the Enemy presents to you. What will you no longer be afraid to fight for? (Refer to your tool options in your survival kit.)

_____

_____

_____

_____

_____

_____

WRITE YOUR OWN PRAYER AND DECLARATION

Prayer

_____

_____

_____

_____

_____

_____

_____

_____

Declaration

_____

_____

_____

_____

_____

_____

_____

_____

NOTES:

CHAPTER 3

TOOLS FOR MAINTAINING YOUR GRACE AND DIGNITY

Food for Thought

Have you ever met anybody who has gone through a life trauma? Perhaps the person experienced death, divorce, abuse, the loss of employment or some other devastating event. One of life's prospects is that we will all face some emotionally disturbing events that will affect us differently. Some people find healthy ways of coping, while others never recover. The situation changes them drastically and diminishes the spiritual fruit they once had.

As believers, we are not exempt from life's hurt and pain. However, with the Lord's help, we can use our traumatic experiences to assist someone else who may be experiencing something similar. We can also show others who have lost hope and are on the verge of giving up that it is possible to survive the trauma and blossom into an even better version of themselves. I admit it is not an easy process to endure, but I also know that with faith, hard work, and determination, you can do it. When you learn to lean on your Lord and Savior Jesus Christ through devastating experiences, He will preserve you and help you navigate through tough times. Our circumstances may not change, but God will change *us* for the better. He will give us supernatural peace for our journey.

🔑 Key Truth #1

Then he told this parable: "A man had a fig tree growing in his vineyard, and he went to look for fruit on it but did not find any. So he said to the man who took care of the vineyard, 'For three years now I've been coming to look for fruit on this fig tree and haven't found any. Cut it down! Why should it use up the soil?' "Sir, the man replied, 'leave it alone for one more year, and I'll dig around it and fertilize it. If it bears fruit next year, fine! If not, then cut it down. (Luke 13:6-8, NIV)

God has a plan for your life. It may not look that way, but trust Him and never doubt what He is doing. He sees your future and knows the magnitude of your victory if you persevere.

🔑 Key Truth #2

Let's examine the necessary steps for restoration. In *Unmute Your Heart,* we talked about the steps necessary to restore a tree to a healthy, fruitful state. Look deep within yourself to understand what you need to apply to your life naturally and spiritually in order to receive the transformation and healing you desire.

We will examine different methods used to restore the health of a tree and parallel them *naturally* and *spiritually*. We will define the **digging around process**, the **relocating process**, the **fertilizing process**, and the **pruning process**.

💡 Survival Kit Question #1

In the Word of God, we are personified as trees. One of the methods used to preserve a tree is the "**digging around**" process. In the natural, this helps to preserve the tree from disease and root decay. Similarly, this process in the spiritual prevents the disease of sin from ultimately destroying us. Spiritual destruction occurs when you don't empty yourself of toxic habits, behaviors, and emotions.

The "**digging around**" process indicates that you still have something to live for; you have a purpose to fulfill.

Write down the goals, dreams, and desires that you want God to restore, resurrect, and breathe life into again.

Survival Kit Question #2

What steps will you take to nurture your goals, dreams, and desires while you are incubating the promises of God? What tools are needed to achieve them?

Core Exercise

The **relocating process** is all about the health, safety, and well-being of the tree. In *Unmute Your Heart,* we talked about the importance of relocating a tree with the root ball attached. We established this was necessary for the successful continued growth of the tree when it is replanted. In the natural, the relocating process represents an emotional, mental, and psychological shift to a safe haven from the terrors of an abusive relationship. The root ball is your testimony of redemption. It signifies growth showing where God has brought you from and where He is taking you.

Before we begin the next portion, let's pray.

Prayer

Lord Jesus, cover every reader in Your precious, saving, healing, and powerful blood. In Your name, we bind and rebuke the spirit of fear and doubt. We replace it with Your love, power, and soundness of mind. We rebuke every spirit of back-lash and retaliation effective immediately. In the matchless name of Jesus. Amen.

🛟 Lifeline

Are you safe in your environment at home or work? If yes, proceed to question number two. If not, seek professional help. If you are thinking about leaving your abusive relationship, here are a few resources you can contact for free domestic abuse help.

- Domestic violence hotline 1-800-799-7233
- verbalabusejournals.com

1. What have you been asking God for that is connected to your health, safety or well-being?

_____

_____

2. Name someone you can trust to pray for you and hold you accountable.

_____

_____

3. Write down the rewards and victories you can receive if you stay focused and push through every tough battle.

_____

_____

💡 Survival Kit Question #3

The **fertilizing process** deals with your spiritual and natural diet. I know you have heard the term, "You are what you eat," so who is pouring into you spiritually? To grow, you must read the Word of God and connect to a ministry where you can be fed. Guard yourself against negative, messy people who will pollute you and stunt your growth.

1. Write down what you can do daily to ensure that you are reading and meditating on God's Word.

_____

_____

2. Write down what you can do daily to ensure that you are praying and spending time with God.

_____

_____

_____

_____

3. Who is in your circle? What kind of appetite do they have? Is it more carnal or spiritual?

_____

_____

_____

_____

4. Do those in your inner circle bring more positive and uplifting energy or do they bring more negative, defeated, and complacent energy around you?

_____

_____

_____

_____

5. Write down the changes and adjustments you need to make so your healing can continue to progress naturally and spiritually.

_____

_____

_____

_____

Survival Kit Question #4

The **pruning process** can be painful, but it is necessary and beneficial. It produces abundant blessings in your life. Pruning a tree involves removing the dead, overgrown stems or branches to increase fruitfulness and growth.

Pruning happens during the winter times of our lives. Winter can represent many things; some good and some bad. However, in the natural, many things die in the winter. What am I saying to you? There comes a time when some of the things we love and enjoy have to be cut off. They can be people, places we go or the things we like to do. To grow and reach a new level of fruitfulness and productivity in God, we have to do some pruning and move forward. When you have had enough of the limitations that have held you hostage for so long, you will do what it takes to get your breakthrough. Life is short and tomorrow is not promised.

1. How many times have you promised yourself you will do better, but you procrastinated time and time again? It is time to start fresh and take one day at a time. List three things you are going to change effective immediately.

   a. _____

   b. _____

   c. _____

2. Evaluate and write down who or what is causing you to remain complacent and not move forward. Explain how.

   _____

   _____

   _____

3. Write down the reasons why you deserve to live in the fruitfulness and abundance of God. What action do you need to take naturally or spiritually to achieve this?

   _____

   _____

   _____

4. There are many ways to be fruitful and live in abundance in your life. Write down specifically what you want to see God do.

🎒 Backpack Tools

Life is full of choices and ever-changing circumstances. They will all test you. You must remember it is just that, a test! Tests are inevitable; they are all part of the transformation process. Abuse will test your strength, confidence, and faith, but if you make up your mind to persevere, you will have enough fight to conquer it all.

Reflect on a time when you were determined to be an overcomer. How did you feel? What backpack tools did you use to help you become a victor? Explain. (Refer to the tool options in your survival kit.)

WRITE YOUR OWN PRAYER AND DECLARATION

🙏 Prayer

Declaration

_____

_____

_____

_____

_____

_____

NOTES:

_____

_____

_____

_____

_____

_____

_____

_____

_____

_____

_____

_____

CHAPTER 4

TOOLS FOR BARBIE

Food for Thought

Beauty is not all about what we look like on the outside. We can easily put fine clothes, expensive jewelry, and red-bottom shoes on a Barbie doll or even slay when it comes to hair and makeup. At the end of the day, no matter how good we look on the outside in our super girl costumes, we can fool others but not ourselves. If we were broken and abused before we put on the fancy stuff, we are still broken and abused hiding behind a mask. We are in need of healing and restoration that only God can give.

Key Truth #1

Living life as a Barbie doll causes a woman to not live out her true identity. You live in a false reality being who everyone else expects you to be. Sad to say, you never really get to know who you are. True freedom allows you to express how you feel and be okay with the healthy decisions you make for your life (in the divine will of God). Let go of the fear that people may have instilled in you. Live unapologetically victorious.

Key Truth #2

In the "Barbie Doll" chapter of *Unmute Your Heart*, we talked about three major senses that Barbie didn't have. Although she had a mouth, eyes, and ears, she was unable to speak, see, and hear.

We are both natural and spiritual. These two elements will be discussed further but before we do, let us earnestly say the following prayer:

Prayer

Lord Jesus, help me to unlock the truths behind my hurts and pains. When I am emotionally and mentally ready, gently reveal the answers to my questions so that truth and healing can be manifested. In Jesus' name, I pray. Amen.

Survival Kit Question #1

1. Describe one or two occasions in your life naturally and spiritually when you wanted something that was neither what you needed nor what was good for you.

   _____

   _____

   _____

2. How did getting that thing affect you naturally?

   _____

   _____

   _____

3. How did getting that thing affect you spiritually?

   _____

   _____

   _____

4. If you could do it over, would you make the same choice? Why or why not?

   In all your ways acknowledge Him, And He shall direct your paths. (Proverbs 3:6)

   _____

   _____

5. Moving forward, what survival kit tool(s) can aid in your decision making process?

_____

_____

⟨?⟩ Survival Kit Question #2

1. Describe an occasion (naturally speaking) when you did not use your voice to advocate for yourself. How did you feel and what was the outcome?

_____

_____

_____

2. Spiritually speaking, describe an occasion where you did not speak life or war in the spirit for yourself; you remained silent. How did you feel and what was the outcome?

_____

_____

_____

3. Knowing what you know now and moving forward as you mature into a more refined woman, how have your experiences shaped you naturally and spiritually?

_____

_____

_____

a. Naturally

_____

_____

b. Spiritually

_____

_____

Survival Kit Question #3

1. Describe an occasion when you heard from God concerning decisions you were contemplating.

   _____

   _____

   _____

2. Describe the outcome when you ignored Him.

   a. Naturally

   _____

   _____

   b. Spiritually

   _____

   _____

3. Describe the outcome when you took heed.

   a. Naturally

   _____

   _____

   b. Spiritually

   _____

   _____

4. How important is it for you to hear from God now? Explain.

   _____

   _____

   _____

5. Have your past mistakes taught you to trust God more? How and why?

_____

_____

_____

_____

_____

_____

Backpack Tools

Indeed, our challenges should make us women of strength and substance – if we allow them to. They enable us to mentor and help other women. Think of someone you know who may be going through a Barbie doll syndrome; she may need a little help or guidance. Make it your assignment to follow up, encourage, and pour into her. Pray for her daily. We need godly, wise, and refined women of God.

Moving forward in this process, what backpack tools can you use in your assignment to help other women? (Refer to the tool options in your survival kit.)

_____

_____

_____

_____

_____

_____

_____

WRITE YOUR OWN PRAYER AND DECLARATION

Prayer

_____

_____

_____

_____

_____

_____

_____

_____

Declaration

_____

_____

_____

_____

_____

_____

_____

_____

CHAPTER 5

TOOLS FOR UNMUTING
YOUR HEART

Food for Thought

Forgive so you can live. There is no other way around it; simply let it go! When we hold people hostage – in our hearts and minds – for things they have done to us, it is like walking around with weights on. It is a heavy burden to bear, and you go nowhere fast. Unforgiveness will eventually consume you. It will make you toxic and bitter from the inside out. It is time to release the toxic emotions of unforgiveness, anger, hatred, bitterness, fear, and doubt. It will take time, but it is possible.

I must share something with you that totally amazed me as a believer. I worked in the prison system in California where we are known for our rehabilitation program for inmates who are incarcerated. One of the programs that really impacted my life was one where we worked with family members of innocent victims who were senselessly murdered or were victims of violent crimes. The many stories are heart-wrenching. The most interesting fact is that some of the family members who once held on to very toxic emotions (unforgiveness, anger and bitterness) recognized the importance of letting go. They realized that in order for them to move forward and regain their lives, healing, as well as freedom, they had to extend forgiveness to those who hurt them and their families.

Forgiveness is powerful; it taught me a very valuable lesson. I learned that when you release what you have no control over, let God be God and deal with the offender you can take back your life. You can be healed and restored through time and patience. Place the burden on God. It is too heavy for you to carry. God can handle it. Let me add that the offender never gets off scot-free. Do not worry about it. Let God handle it. Your job is to prayerfully take back your life, be healed and restored, so you can live again.

Key Truth #1

A brother offended is harder to be won than a strong city: and their contentions are like the bars of a castle. (Proverbs 18:19, KJV)

This passage is very powerful yet disturbing at the same time. It addresses the fact that in many cases, it can be very difficult to forgive someone who was close to you that has offended you. Hence, there are major divisions making it almost impossible for reconciliation because of bitterness and quarrels. Let your prayer to God be for godly repentance and forgiveness. Allow His love to flow through you like a river of healing, so you may live in true peace.

Prayer

Heavenly Father, please cover my heart and mind in Your precious blood. Help me to forgive quickly so that no seeds of bitterness, envy or strife will take root in my heart. Help me to possess a spirit of love understanding and reconciliation for my own good, health and well-being. In Jesus name, amen.

Survival Kit Question #1

What hindrances are you currently facing that are keeping you from forgiving those who offended you?

_____

_____

_____

_____

Survival Kit Question #2

Who are you holding unforgiveness against that is keeping you from receiving forgiveness from God?

_____

_____

Core Exercise

Search your heart. Have you truly forgiven those who have hurt you?

_____

_____

Do you avoid those who have offended you? Explain why.

_____

_____

Does your heart race when you see the offender? If so, why?

_____

_____

Does your emotional state change if the offender is around? If so, explain what happens and why.

_____

_____

Are you constantly consumed with what the person did/said? If so, explain why.

_____

_____

_____

Do you want to hurt certain individuals who have offended you? If so, explain why.

_____

_____

_____

Do you feel justified to harbor toxic emotions against someone who has offended you? Why or why not?

_____

_____

_____

If you have answered yes to any of these questions, explain truthfully to yourself how it has impacted your life positively or negatively.

_____

_____

_____

Key Truth #2

Remember to always watch your motives and stay focused on your healing process. Allow God to handle the rest.

> He that covereth his sins shall not prosper: but whosoever confesseth and forsaketh them shall have mercy. (Proverbs 28:13, KJV)

> Rejoice not when thine enemy falleth, and let not thine heart be glad when he stumbleth. (Proverbs 24:17, KJV)

There are many ways to harbor unforgiveness in your heart. Beware because unforgiveness produces evil seeds like the ones listed below. If you are not careful, they will take root and grow.

- Lack of mercy
- Judgmental behavior
- Resentment
- Slander
- Vengeance
- Retaliation
- Bitterness

The list goes on. Forgiving others does not mean you have to reestablish a relationship with those who have offended you. It simply means that you are extending the gift of grace to your offender. This is something that is not deserved, but just as Jesus did for us when He died for our sins, we are to extend mercy. We don't deserve it, but by His lovingkindness, grace, and mercy we obtain the gift of eternal life. Forgiveness is for your recovery. It helps you to regain a newness of life.

Backpack Tools

We must truly put everything that keeps us from progressing before the Lord. You would be surprised at some of the things people try to convince themselves they are free from. In actuality, they are afraid to see how ugly and bound they really are. They justify their actions to let themselves off the hook. If this is you, now is the time to bring every thought into captivity to the obedience of Christ, so you can receive the truth and be free.

In moving forward, what survival tools can help you to excel and experience true freedom? (Refer to the tool options in your survival kit.)

_____

_____

_____

_____

_____

WRITE YOUR OWN PRAYER AND DECLARATION

Prayer

_____

_____

_____

_____

_____

_____

_____

_____

Declaration

_____

_____

_____

_____

_____

_____

_____

_____

CHAPTER 6

TOOLS FOR FINE TUNING YOUR HEARING

Food for Thought

Have you ever heard a song or melody that was so beautiful you wanted to hear it over and over again? Or have you ever listened to a seasoned man or woman of God share sound wisdom or instruction that enlightened and guided you through a difficult season? Have you ever heard a word from the Lord that settled your heart and mind? It gave you so much peace and confidence that you knew in the midst of your trial, everything was going to be okay. If ever you need a word from the Lord, it is now! The only way to hear clearly from God is through a relationship with Him and being filled with His precious Holy Spirit.

> Likewise the Spirit also helpeth our infirmities: for we know not what we should pray for as we ought: but the Spirit itself maketh intercession for us with groanings which cannot be uttered. (Romans 8:26, KJV)

As we continue to pray, read His Word, and stay in fellowship, God will reveal secrets and mysteries to His children. He will keep us abreast of what we need to know concerning our families, jobs, and direction for our lives. We must stay connected to the power source, the one who holds tomorrow, sees our future, and knows the steps that we should take. He makes no mistakes.

What happens when He tells us something that we don't want to hear? Do we continue to trust Him? Yes, we do. However, we must also pray for the grace to accept what He allows knowing He is the sovereign God.

🔑 Key Truth #1

We must obey the Word and the leading of the Lord. Jonah is a perfect example of what happens when we do things our way. God told Jonah to go to Nineveh and cry against it. Instead, Jonah fled to Tarshish because he felt the people of Nineveh didn't deserve to be warned by God. He was convinced they should have been punished. While he was at sea, a storm came; his disobedience put others on the boat at risk. He knew it was his disobedience that caused the trouble. Subsequently, he repented and obeyed God (Jonah chapters 1-4).

Another story I love is found in Isaiah 38:3-5. Hezekiah was sick unto death. The prophet Isaiah visited Hezekiah with a message from the Lord to set his house in order because he was going to die. The Bible says Hezekiah turned his face toward the wall and prayed unto the Lord. Hezekiah was faithful; hence he could ask God to change His mind and let him live longer. God honored Hezekiah's request and extended his life by 15 more years.

In both stories, God shows grace and mercy. We see the importance of obedience and living a life of faithfulness when serving God. Our lives can be our testimonies, just as Hezekiah's was. God will reward you in ways that only He can.

🔑 Key Truth #2

THE IMPORTANCE OF HEARING

> Then shalt thou kill the ram, and take of his blood, and put it upon the tip of the right ear of Aaron, and upon the tip of the right ear of his sons, and upon the thumb of their right hand, and upon the great toe of their right foot, and sprinkle the blood upon the altar round about. (Exodus 29:20)

In the Old Testament, Moses was commanded by God to anoint the right ear, right thumb, and right big toe of Aaron and his sons. I particularly want to point out the right ear and why this was done. It was for listening purposes. Many times, God told Moses and Aaron to do things that seemed ridiculous. Their right ears had to be anointed to ensure they were hearing from God and not be afraid to obey whatever He asked them to do. So it is with us today. We should anoint our ears for listening purposes to know when we are hearing from God, rather than vacillating and wondering whether we are hearing from Him or not. God proves His power through our obedience.

Survival Kit Question #1

Listening to the voice of the Lord through His Word can keep us from many pitfalls. We can hear God's warnings. Recall a time when your obedience blessed your life.

_____

_____

_____

_____

Survival Kit Question #2

Have you ever wanted to do the opposite of what was right knowing it wasn't God's will for your life? How did it play out? Would you do it again the same way? Why or why not?

_____

_____

_____

_____

Core Exercise

Blind faith is when we pray and hope for the best to come out of difficult circumstances. We cannot see how it is possible through our natural eyes, so we must be obedient and patient while waiting on God. Make a prayer list of the things in your life you have to trust and hear from God about because you can't see the end result.

PRAYER LIST

1. _____

2. _____

3. _____

4. _____

5. _____

Backpack Tools

Perhaps, you have made impulsive decisions without hearing from God because of your fleshly desires. Moving forward, what backpack survival kit tools can help you experience a favorable outcome with added blessings when you listen and hear directly from God? Explain. (Refer to the tool options in your survival kit.)

_____

_____

_____

WRITE YOUR OWN PRAYER AND DECLARATION

Prayer

_____

_____

_____

_____

_____

_____

Declaration

NOTES:

NOTES:

CHAPTER 7

TOOLS TO KEEP YOU SHINING LIKE A STAR

☀ Food for Thought

What you think about yourself will manifest outwardly. What God knows about us when He formed us in the womb is far greater than what we know. If we want to remain free from all the satanic attacks that come to keep us bound, we must realize who we are in God and agree with His Word concerning us. Often, we allow the important people in our lives to build us up or tear us down. Either way, we tend to agree with what they say because we hold them in high regard. We let them have the final say.

In the chapter titled "Star" of *Unmute Your Heart*, I talk about how my ex mentally and emotionally abused me with his false accusations, lies, degradation, and assassination of my character. I was crushed from the inside out. My heart and soul were deeply wounded and I sank into a depression.

One day, after being in a serious car accident and suffering from tremendous injuries to my head and shoulder, God began to deal with me about the scar from the accident that was left on my forehead. He told me that it was to be named a "star." As I pondered this in my mind, the Lord revealed to me that it represented the fact Jesus can turn our emotional scars into stars and identify us as His own. This is exactly what He did for me. No longer did I have to be emotionally wounded by what someone else was thinking or speaking about me. I could be free from that burden.

In the book, I talk about how God showed me a horse in a vision and how the discoloration in the middle of the horse's head has many names. However, the name He pointed out to me was "star." The pattern of the discoloration is different on every horse making it easier for an owner to identify his horse should it become lost or stolen. No one else can claim it because only the owner would know his horse by its star. This works much like a diamond that has certain coal specs, patterns or designs within it. The jeweler maps it out so that if it is ever stolen, lost, and found, it would have a unique pattern or design that only the owner would have knowledge of to claim what is rightfully his.

Likewise, the Father knows His children who belong to Him. We stand out because we are different. God loves and cares for us above anything that anyone could ever think or say about us negatively. He knows what is in our hearts, our intentions, and our motives.

God's love can shine through you. People can see the beauty of your heart. God can give you peace and freedom from all mental and emotional traumas. He is more than able to change your negative mindset, stagnant situations, and circumstances for your health and healing. Everybody's freedom does not look the same. There are many ways to freedom and one is designed specifically for your situation. Now that you understand the fact that belonging to God means He wants us to be totally healed and free.

🔑 Key Truth #1

You can only receive your freedom when you are honest with God and yourself, if you truly want it, and you are willing to do the hard work to receive your desired outcome. Now let us examine our freedom.

💪 Core Exercise

Read the end of the chapter "Star" in *Unmute Your Heart* that is duplicated below. Write down the various types of freedom **you** need to receive from God. After you have done so, write down the importance of that particular freedom for your life personally.

- The ultimate freedom is His *redemption*. He redeemed us by gaining possession of His people in exchange for His life. The debt of sin was cleared through His powerful blood
- His *deliverance* power is experienced when He rescues us from the power of Satan and sets us free from sin

- Some people are in need of *liberation*. The act of being liberated is when a person(s) has been set free from imprisonment, slavery, oppression, confinement, and bondage
- Maybe you need to be *discharged*. Some of us need to tell someone or ourselves that we can or must leave a place or situation
- *Release* – Some of us need to allow God to help us escape the confinements of Satan and be set free from bondage; this is what God did for me personally, and I no longer have to carry that emotional burden. He released me
- Some of us need to be *rescued* from dangerous or distressing situations. I have found that when people have been in abusive situations, it is hard for them to make healthy decisions for themselves because of fear. Sometimes they feel obligated to stay in the torment because of financial concerns, children or even to maintain a reputation. However, they need to be rescued, and they must know that. Those of us who have relationships with Jesus Christ have the ability to save lives. We must render assistance to those who do not understand there is a better way
- *Emancipation* – This is the process of being set free from legal, social or political restrictions. Some of us need freedom from the court system. It is overtaxing, overwhelming, and stressful, but our God is able to deliver

Whatever you need to be set free from in your life, God is here to do it. We no longer have to live under the burden of the law. Instead, we can live under the authority and power of God.

> For God sent not his Son into the world to condemn the world; but that the world through him might be saved. (John 3:17)

Identify areas in which you need to be free and their importance in your life.

_____

_____

_____

_____

_____

_____

⟨?⟩ Survival Kit Question #1

With the truth of His Word and a strategic plan, God can change our lives, and we can walk in freedom. Moving forward, how do you see yourself in the future?

_____

_____

_____

🎒 Backpack Tools

To shine like a star and maintain a healthy outlook, we must feel good about ourselves. We must understand that God loves us, and we belong to Him. Every negative thought the Enemy tries to plant in our minds can be destroyed by the power of God. What survival kit tool(s) can help you fortify your mind, maintain your peace, and keep all negative suggestions from the Enemy about you eradicated? Explain. (Refer to the tool options in your survival kit.)

_____

_____

WRITE YOUR OWN PRAYER AND DECLARATION

🙏 Prayer

_____

_____

_____

_____

_____

_____

Declaration

NOTES:

NOTES:

CHAPTER 8

TOOLS FOR PROTECTING OUR CHILDREN

Food for Thought

Unfortunately, many adults are the end-products of their traumatic childhoods; their growth has been stunted. As a result of childhood trauma, many people create defense mechanisms to prevent them from ever being hurt or violated by others again. Some children grow into scared, wounded adults whose hearts, minds, and spirits have been scarred. They never got healing for their hurts. In many cases, they have never received any professional or spiritual counseling and have suppressed emotions that may be triggered by events later in life. Believe it or not, even the trauma that parents experience as adults if we are not careful will be passed on to our children. They see us as examples of how to deal with life issues. If we are toxic, bitter, and angry, chances are our children may pick up the same toxic emotions. Why? Because they have no example of what they should do or how they should handle traumatic experiences in life. My traumatic experiences were divorce and abuse, so I will address those issues in this chapter.

As parents, I found that it was very important to model healthy ways of dealing with divorce when our children are caught in the crossfire. However, I had never experienced my parents going through a divorce so I had to figure a lot of things out on my own. On the other hand, my ex's parents were divorced and he could only draw from what he know. As a result, in some ways he responded according to his experience. We as parents must receive professional help to heal from our past experiences and learn new, positive ways to cope especially when there are children involved. When we seek help we are able to be good examples for our children. It is going to be hard no matter what because they don't have a say so in the matter. Divorce is like death for some people. It is destructive, particularly when there has been years of emotional investment, time spent, children involved and assets to be divided; it can be a mess. Let's not mention the open lack of respect toward one another, which can be devastating. Thank God He knows all about what we go through and He can cover our children through the toughest of times.

As arrows are in the hand of a mighty man; so are children of the youth. (Psalm 127:4)

We must not plant negative seeds in our children's hearts against the other parent. Instead, we should teach them right from wrong and to be aware of what is good and bad. Like an arrow in our hands, they will go in whatever direction we aim them. Children tend to find out what they need to know and can move forward. They may not be happy about the details, but hopefully, they will learn something valuable along the way. If you plant negative seeds in your children's hearts, they will harbor unforgiveness and nurture roots of bitterness. Your disease will become their disease. It is a hard pill to swallow, but we must learn to trust God to handle and work out the details of every situation.

Key Truth #1

Train up a child in the way he should go: and when he is old, he will not depart from it. (Proverbs 22:6, KJV)

As parents, we must remember to do our part and allow God to do the rest.

Survival Kit Question #1

Parents do the best we can in most cases; however, because we are only human, we make mistakes sometimes. What is one major thing you can change right now to build a better relationship with your children (young or adults)?

_____

_____

_____

Survival Kit Question #2

In what ways can we help guard our children's hearts and minds when dealing with tough challenges that impact them directly?

_____

_____

_____

Survival Kit Question #3

Nobody comes from a perfect family. Knowing your family background and upbringing, what generational curses do you want to believe God to break and destroy from the lives of your children?

_____

_____

_____

_____

Backpack Tools

Moving forward, what tools can you use while praying and interceding for your children who have experienced the crossfire? (Refer to the tool options in your survival kit.)

_____

_____

_____

_____

WRITE YOUR OWN PRAYER AND DECLARATION

Prayer

_____

_____

_____

_____

_____

_____

_____

_____

Declaration

_____

_____

_____

_____

_____

_____

_____

_____

CHAPTER

TOOLS FOR SURVIVING YOUR SEASONS

Food for Thought

In the movie *Forrest Gump*, the main character Forrest Gump said, "Life is like a box of chocolates. You never know what you're gonna get." Life is full of swift transitions: good, bad, happy or sad. You can find yourself in circumstances you never thought possible. One event can shake the core of your reality and change the rest of your life instantly.

Seasons change, and we are eager to get through the hard ones as quickly as possible. In some cases, the only thing left to do is accept the situation and live with the outcome. Often, we find it hard to move forward when something has hurt us or affected our lives drastically. This brings us to a fork in the road, and we are uncertain whether to choose fight or flight.

If you fight, you make the choice to push forward, live again, and learn something valuable to help others if you can. If you choose to take flight, you will potentially accept the worst with detrimental results that hold you hostage to fear and defeat. Whatever season of your life you are experiencing, remember we serve a God who can change the times and seasons. He will walk with you through the toughest times giving you real joy and peace in the midst of any storm.

And he changeth the times and the seasons: he removeth kings, and setteth up kings: he giveth wisdom unto the wise, and knowledge to them that know understanding. (Daniel 2:21, KJV)

🔑 Key Truth #1

To everything there is a season, and a time to every purpose under the heaven: A time to be born, and a time to die; a time to plant, and a time to pluck up that which is planted; A time to kill, and a time to heal; a time to break down, and a time to build up; A time to weep, and a time to laugh; a time to mourn, and a time to dance. (Ecclesiastes 3:1-4)

Through every season of our lives, God will be there even when it gets hard, and we want to quit. He knows how much we can bear. Just hold on to your faith and trust Him to see you through.

❓ Survival Kit Question #1

How can you honor God when things are good in your life? How can you honor God when things are bad and not looking favorable for you?

_____

_____

_____

❓ Survival Kit Question #2

What can you do when you are waiting on God and you hear nothing? How can you build your trust and faith in Him?

_____

_____

_____

_____

_____

Survival Kit Backpack

As you move forward, what tool option(s) should you use when you are faced with uncertainty about the outcome of your season?

Let not your heart be troubled: ye believe in God, believe also in me. (John 14:1, KJV)

_____

_____

_____

_____

_____

_____

WRITE YOUR OWN PRAYER AND DECLARATION

Prayer

_____

_____

_____

_____

_____

_____

_____

🗩 Declaration

_____

_____

_____

_____

_____

_____

_____

NOTES:

_____

_____

_____

_____

_____

_____

_____

_____

_____

_____

_____

CHAPTER 10

TOOLS FOR DECLARING YOUR VICTORY

Food for Thought

What does the Enemy know that he doesn't want you to know? That you have the power to speak and declare those things that are not as though they are. There is power in what we speak. We can speak life or we can speak death because whatever we speak will bear the fruit thereof.

> Death and life are in the power of the tongue: and they that love it shall eat the fruit thereof. (Proverbs 18:21, KJV)

We must speak life even to our circumstances that seem to be dead. Sometimes after encountering difficult challenges, you are drained of energy. There is no real joy or peace and you literally feel as if you are barely hanging on by a thread. Nevertheless, I admonish you to keep pushing forward. Speak life into yourself again. Take the time to care for you. Use your voice to praise God and declare that the worst is over; the best is yet to come. Remember to always pray for God's perfect will to be done in your life. You will be confident things will be okay when you let God have total control over your circumstances.

🔑 Key Truth #1

I felt I had to accept every abusive word that was spoken because my ex-husband's words seemed to be way more powerful than mine. But that was a lie from the Enemy. The more I became free in my mind to believe and trust the Word of God, the more strength I gained. I used the power of my voice to move a great big God on my behalf. I encourage you to start building your faith even more in the Word of God. Agree with His truth through the Word.

> Nay, in all these things we are more than conquerors through him that loved us. (Romans 8:37, KJV)

❓ Survival Kit Question #1

Living to speak and declare puts a continual action in motion as you live daily. What positive words will you speak over your life daily? What positive things will you declare over your life daily?

_____

_____

_____

💗 Core Exercise

Be mindful every day to think, speak, and declare only positive things in your life and the lives of those around you. Change your outlook on life and about yourself. *Think* of things that are positive and uplifting that will help keep you in good spirits – things that are happy and inspiring. *Speak* things that are kind and wholesome that free your spirit and encourage you, as well as others around you to thrive. No matter the challenges you may face, *declare* to the Enemy and yourself that it is well. Stand on that declaration with the power and authority given by God.

1. Write down five positive things you *think* about yourself.

  a. _____

  b. _____

c. _____

d. _____

e. _____

2. Write down five positive things you will *speak* about yourself.

   a. _____

   b. _____

   c. _____

   d. _____

   e. _____

3. Write down five positive things you will *declare* over your life.

   a. _____

   b. _____

   c. _____

   d. _____

   e. _____

Backpack Tools

We must be mindful to declare the promises of God when the opposition says differently. What spiritual tools can we use to build our confidence that we can be victorious? (Refer to the tool options in the survival kit.)

_____

_____

_____

_____

_____

_____

WRITE YOUR OWN PRAYER AND DECLARATION

Prayer

_____

_____

_____

_____

_____

_____

_____

_____

Declaration

_____

_____

_____

_____

_____

_____

_____

_____

_____

CHAPTER

TOOLS FOR UNLOCKING YOUR SECRETS

Food for Thought

In this chapter of *Unmute Your Heart*, I discover through honesty that I secretly desired to be in a relationship with my ex again. I felt like it could have been the right thing to do because after all, he was the father of my children. I wanted to keep my family together at any cost despite what I had encountered. I wanted my family to "look right" knowing that it would be the worst mistake to make.

It was revealed to me that my little secret was ultimately holding me back from moving forward. The crazy thing was I felt I had no options. Who would want a woman with five kids? I constantly found myself between a rock and a hard place. I would rehash the traumatic abuse I suffered, the hurtful and degrading things that were said and done. I would cry because I couldn't understand what I did to deserve such bad treatment. I was always trying to figure things out.

Ultimately, I had not let my ex go. It was a 20-year soul tie that was being torn apart, and I was hurting. I was trapped in a state of denial. People would ask me if I still loved him and if given the chance, would I salvage things between us. My answer was always "no".

Our divorce was on display for all to see because he was a Pastor and an ex NFL football player with influence. My character was publicly assassinated and it took much counseling and prayer just for me to recover from the mental and emotional trauma. I would be considered a fool if I had confessed that I wanted to go back to the very man whose fabrications soiled my name. The conflicting truth was that in my heart I did still love him, and I did want things to work between us. I would constantly pray and convince myself he would change as an excuse to return to him. However, if I had decided to go back to him, it would have been a grave mistake. I needed to heal, empty myself, and learn my own value and self-worth.

I believe in marriage and reconciliation, but I don't condone abuse of any kind. Marriage requires the work of two people. If one is willing to get counseling, while the other party is not interested, stubborn or too proud to admit that help is needed then that is definitely something you must take to the Lord in prayer. Let God speak to you. Sadly, too many lives have been lost because the dangerous signs of abusive behavior were ignored or overlooked. As a result of this, many women have lost the ability to know how to live meaningful lives; others have lost the chance to live.

> The heart is deceitful above all things, and desperately wicked: who can know it? (Jeremiah 17:9)

Our hearts will deceive us frequently simply because we don't trust that God has everything under control. Our low self-esteem and insecurities make us feel as if we are of no value. We settle into what's familiar because we're afraid of change. However, when we walk in God's plan for our lives and delight ourselves in Him, our focus turns to Him, and He can reward us with our hearts' desires. We are not always right about the things we believe are best for us. I would rather trust God who holds my future and knows what is best for me.

🔑 Key Truth #1

> But seek ye first the kingdom of God, and his righteousness; and all these things shall be added unto you. (Matthew 6:33, KJV)

There are many things that we seek after in this life; we pursue our careers, our goals, our dreams and our education. But the most important thing that we can ever seek after is God. Many times, we feel that there are things that we want which are of great importance to us. However, when we are truly seeking the face of God our desires may even change. The Lord will set us on a course to fulfill the desires of our hearts when we least expect it simply because we put Him first. I am not saying that it is wrong to pursue after what you want, what I am saying is to make sure that God is your number one priority.

Usually, God has already shown us His plan and purpose for our lives. If you have been following His plan for your life, remain focused and on task. If you are not doing God's will, ask Him to open your eyes in the natural and spiritual for a clear revelation.

💡 Survival Kit Question #1

Seeking God is the key to receiving your heart's desire (according to His will). However, if you have been focused on the wrong things, how will you turn your situation around? Are you doing the will of God for your life?

_____

_____

_____

_____

💡 Survival Kit Question #2

What's in your heart that you want to confess so that you can make things right with God? What do you need to uproot and pluck out to receive complete deliverance?

_____

_____

_____

_____

💗 Core Exercise

Stop what you are doing. Close your eyes and meditate on the question above. Ask God to show you daily how to release and let go of anything that you may find difficult to let go of. Next, I want you to write down your answers in the heart diagram below. Pray daily for deliverance and release from past, present, and even future hurts that may be triggered from your past. You may even realize that you need further help through counseling. As you begin to heal and release those toxic emotions, guard your heart and mind against the Enemy as he tries to keep you bound. One of his tactics is telling you that you cannot be free. However, as you keep giving the burden of bondage to God, your freedom will manifest.

_____

_____

_____

Write your answers inside the heart.

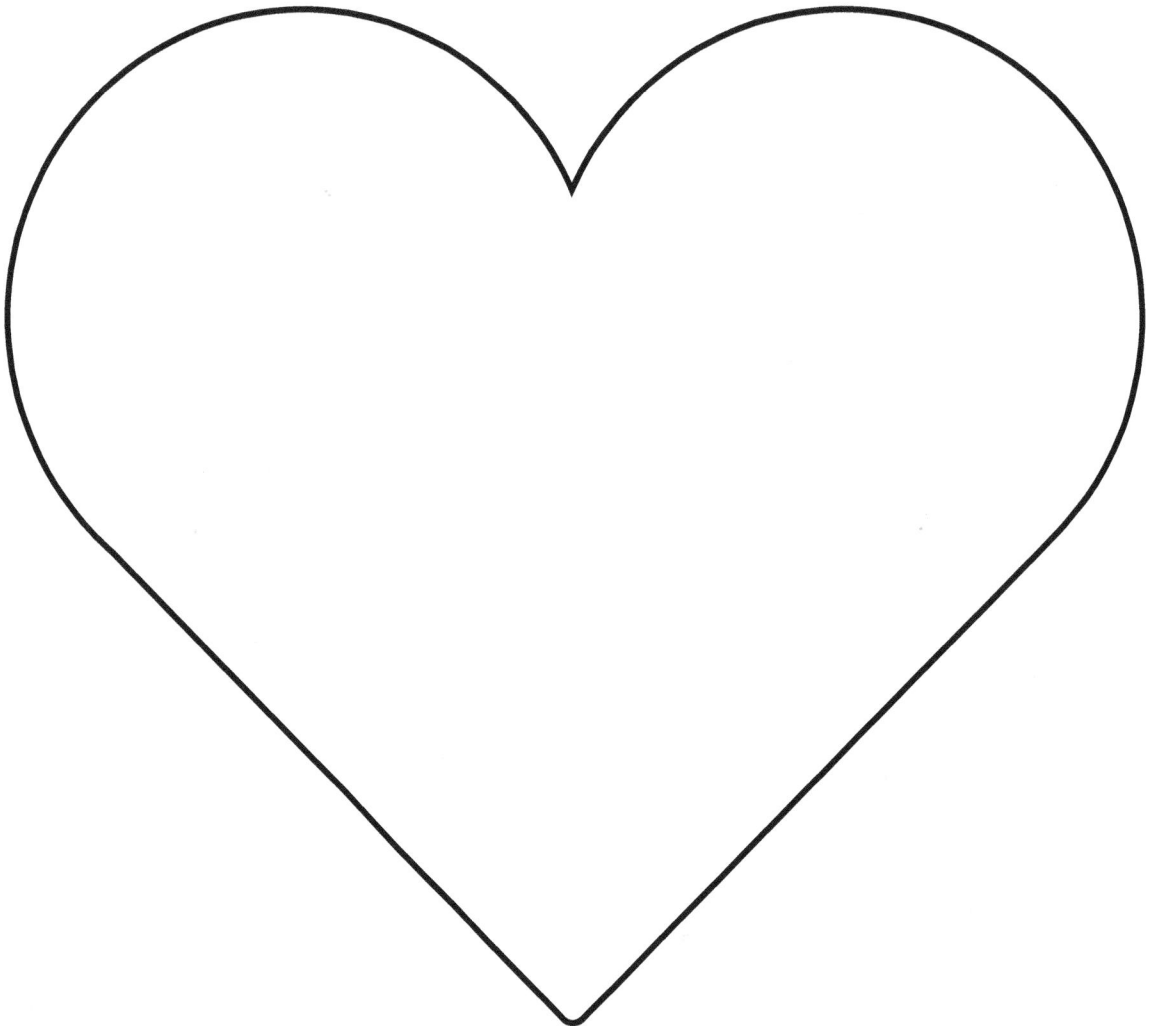

And the peace of God, which passeth all understanding, shall keep your hearts and minds through Christ Jesus. (Philippians 4:7, KJV)

Your heart will dictate your actions. Guard it. Be careful what you think because it will manifest outwardly.

Backpack Tools

Moving forward, what tools can you use to keep a healthy heart and mind? How can you overcome when the Enemy says you can't be free to live, love, forgive, and heal? How do you deal with the doubt he creates in your mind? (Refer back to the tool options in the survival kit.)

_____

_____

_____

You can only be accountable for you and your actions. You must forgive yourself and others to move forward. You are not responsible for anyone who chooses not to forgive you. Walk in the new freedom you have found. Expect great things from God that will take your life to the next level. In Jesus' name, Amen.

WRITE YOUR OWN PRAYER AND DECLARATION

Prayer

_____

_____

_____

_____

_____

_____

_____

_____

Declaration

_____

_____

_____

_____

_____

_____

_____

NOTES:

_____

_____

_____

_____

_____

_____

_____

_____

CHAPTER 12

TOOLS FOR PRAYING FOR YOUR CHILDREN

Food for Thought

It is very important that we continue to pray for our children no matter how old they are. As believers, we must teach and train them according to the Word of God and trust God to do the rest. I have experienced some heartache, disappointment, and sleepless nights due to choices that some of my children have made. As parents, we want the best for our children, but sometimes they stray from the path we were leading them on. We must continue to teach them God's Word and believe it will prevail and manifest in their lives.

I once heard someone say that when our children are young, they are on our laps, but when they are grown, they are on our hearts. That is true. Our children must also be accountable for their own actions and learn some tough lessons. We must remain prayerful and cast our cares on God, so we can receive His peace when the tough, rocky times show up. Stand on the Word of God for your children's salvation and healing. We can't live our children's lives or make choices for them, but we know the one who holds their future.

One day, my mother lost her daughter, and my siblings and I lost our baby sister Rachel due to health issues (which we knew she had since birth). She was a walking miracle because she looked and acted like someone with a clean bill of health. At 19 years of age, she passed, unexpectedly.

She was a vibrant outgoing college student who worked for the IRS and was engaged to be married. It was a very exciting time in life for her. But it wasn't meant to be. I observed how my mother (an amazing woman in my life) handled that entire situation and the death of my father 10 years earlier. She always trusted God and taught us to pray that His will would be done in every situation. She instilled in us that no matter what, our God is faithful and still a healer. He is sovereign, and we will still serve Him because through it all, God has been good. Of course, my mother and my family were devastated and hurting, but God comforted all of our hearts. He gave us reasons to worship Him and give Him all the glory. My mother taught us to keep moving forward and through the tough times, to stay connected to God. Each day, we draw closer to Him because He is our help in times of distress.

Key Truth #1

> Be careful for nothing; but in everything by prayer and supplication with thanksgiving let your requests be made known unto God. (Philippians 4:6, KJV)

Raising children can be challenging for some people especially for some parents whose children may be rebellious and curious about life and willing to take risks. No matter what your children may be facing or the choices that they may choose to make, we can make our requests made known unto God on their behalf thanking God in advance for the victory.

Core Exercise

Write down the names of your children, grandchildren, godchildren or any children you are standing in the gap for. Commit to praying for them daily. Make your requests known. Call their names out. If they are physically out of reach, pray that God will raise up a man or woman of God nearby to influence their lives. Someone can minister to them wherever they are and plant the seeds of salvation, encouragement, joy, and a desire to call on God in their hearts. Pray that they will draw closer to God and receive whatever it is they need from Him.

PRAYER WALL

💡 Survival Kit Question

Being a parent, we can only do the best we can. Let's face it, we are human, and we make mistakes. Based on this fact, what are some ways you can improve your relationships with your young or adult children (i.e. communication, mutual respect, etc.)?

_____

_____

_____

_____

_____

Backpack Tools

It is apparent that there is no perfect family background and upbringing. What generational curses need to be broken and destroyed from the lives of your children? What tools do you need while you are praying patiently waiting for God to manifest change in their lives? (Refer to the tool options in the survival kit.)

_____

_____

_____

_____

WRITE YOUR OWN PRAYER AND DECLARATION

Prayer

_____

_____

_____

_____

_____

_____

_____

_____

_____

_____

Declaration

_____

_____

_____

_____

_____

_____

_____

_____

NOTES:

_____

_____

_____

_____

_____

_____

_____

_____

NOTES:

www.ingramcontent.com/pod-product-compliance
Lightning Source LLC
Chambersburg PA
CBHW081521040426

42447CB00013B/3291